Cyber Security
&
Accounting
Information Systems

Stay ahead of the technology curve

Y.K.Wong, Ph.D.

Production:

Book submission: 15 June 2016

Book revision: 17 Oct 2016

Final acceptance: 30 Nov 2016

First editorial services submission: 3 Dec 2016

Second editorial services submission: 15 Dec 2016

Cover image: 18 Dec 2016

Online version: 18 Dec 2016

Print version: 10 Jan 2017

Description

With fast growth in information technologies, as well as an increasing number of mobile and wireless devices and services, the need to address vulnerabilities has been highly prioritized by many large corporations, as well as small and medium companies. The value of financial data in an accounting information system is extremely high. Thus, cybersecurity has become a critical concern in managing accounting information systems. Accounting information systems (AIS) aim to support all accounting functions and activities, including financial reporting, auditing, taxation, and management accounting. The AIS is a core knowledge area for accounting professionals and is a critical requirement for accounting practice. This book provides the essential knowledge for the accounting professional to stay ahead of the technology curve. This includes the accounting information system's characteristics, accounting cycles, and accounting processes; reviews different types of information system designs and architectures; and discusses cyber security, vulnerabilities, cybercrime, cyber-attacks, and defense strategies.

Keywords: accounting, information system, cyber security, vulnerability, defense

About the Author

Y.K. Wong, Ph.D.

Y.K. Wong holds a Ph.D. in Computing Science from the University of Technology, Sydney, Australia. She received her Master's degree in Advanced Information Systems and Management from The University of New South Wales, Australia, and a Bachelor of Commerce from Curtin University of Technology, Australia.

Dr. Wong has produced quality publications (books, journals, and referred conference papers). Her first book, titled 'Modern Software Review: Techniques and Technology', was published in 2006. She is the Associate Editor for the International Review of Business Research and the International Journal of PIE (an A-list journal), consulting editor for Australian Journal on Information Systems, and reviewer (scholarly peer-reviewed) for many top-tier journals such as IEEE, AIS, and various A-list journals. She served in the Technical Committee for International Association of Science and Technology for Development between 2006 and 2009, the Academic Advocate for ISACA between 2013 and 2015, and the program and track chairs for several conferences such as the Global Business and Social Science Research Conference in 2014 and Pacific Asia Conference on Information Systems in 2008. She has been actively engaged with professional bodies including the Association for Information Systems Special Interest Group on IT/IS in Asia Pacific (AIS-SIG IT/IS), The International of Association for Accounting Education and Research (IAAER), Project Management Institute (PMI), Academy of Management (AOM), The Information Systems Audit and Control Association (ISACA), IEEE Communications Society (IEEE Communication), ACM Special Interest Group: Mobile (SIG Mobile), and Certified Public Accounting (CPA).

Dr. Wong is a consultant, researcher, and teacher in various universities and international companies. She taught at the

University of New South Wales, Griffith University, the University of Technology, Sydney, and the University of Southern Queensland in the areas of business and information technology between 2001 and 2014. She has been teaching Accounting Information Systems and Auditing since 2010. Prior to her academic appointments, she worked in the areas of enterprise resources planning systems implementation systems and business processes re-engineering, e-commerce solutions, logistics, operations, and procurement; sales and marketing and product development since 1991.

Contents

Chapter 1

Accounting Information Systems

Accounting information systems (AIS) are designed for small to large enterprise businesses. Accounting professionals provide several types of support, including accounting operations (e.g., transaction processing, accounts receivable and payable, and internal reporting), external reporting (e.g., statutory reporting, corporate finance, financial risk, regulation and compliance with regulations, audit, and taxes), strategic accounting management (e.g., forecasting, budgeting, costing, reporting, cash flow management, financial performance, strategic decision supports, benchmarking, and various accounting-related managing activities) (Collier, 2015).

Since AIS have been widely adopted in the last two decades, the trend of accounting practice has shifted from traditional accounting operational support to strategic and control management. The accounting practice trend further concentrates the risks and security controls after the 2008 financial crisis. The results from a survey conducted by Chartered Institute Management Accounting in early 2010 to benchmark the accounting practice worldwide (Stede and Malone, 2010) suggested three major categories of accounting operations: transaction processing, accounting operations, and accounts payable and receivable. Internal and external reporting have been computerized using accounting information systems. More companies now use accounting information systems for accounting operations and transaction processing support, and as such, the demand of financial accounting roles has been reduced.

With the wide adoption of accounting information systems and Computer Assisted Auditing Tools and Techniques (CAATTs), better risk management and controls can be carried out by auditors (Mayberry, 2013). Nowadays, auditors can continuously monitor accounting activities such as errors, fraud detection, analytical data reporting, and interactive reporting. The trend accounting practices has towards strategic accounting management support and auditing focuses on ways to improve the efficiency and effectiveness of audit procedures, risk management, and controls.

What is an Accounting Information System?

An AIS aims to collect, process, store, and report financial data that can be used by managers, accountants, tax agencies, shareholders, and any other internal and external parties for decision making (Fawcett and Martin, 2016). The AIS is a core knowledge area in the accounting discipline and is an important requirement for accounting practice. AISs can be used to support all accounting functions and activities, including financial reporting, auditing, taxation, and management accounting.

AISs were introduced in the early 1970s for payroll functions. At the time, many accounting functions were executed manually, which could be ineffective and inefficient. AISs automate the processing of large amounts of data and produce timely and accurate information. Nowadays, two widely adopted accounting modules using AISs are auditing and financial reporting. With the advanced and rapid growth of information technology and process improvements, the AISs can provide full services to support all functional areas of financial accounting, managerial (management) accounting, taxation, and auditing.

The main components of an AIS are data, software, information technology infrastructure, and internal controls. Procedures and instructions can be automated. By adopting middleware, analytic tools, and user-friendly computer-interface designs, users (e.g., accountants and managers) can easily retrieve accounting information from an AIS.

The accounting functions give measurements, processing and communicating financial information about the business entities. As such, AISs are computerized to support a full range of accounting functions. Understanding business cycles and processes is critical to the success of the accounting functions.

Characteristics of Accounting Information Systems

Key characteristics of AISs are (Collier, 2015; Fawcett and Martin, 2016; Romney and Steinbart, 2016; Fang and Shu, 2016):

- AISs capture data and produce financial statements and reports. This process generally refers to the transaction processing system, which deals with day-to-day business transactions and operations.

- AISs produce financial information that can be used for both external and internal users. The internal users are business managers, who use the accounting information for planning, budgeting, and controls, while external users are customers, shareholders, vendors, investors, stock exchanges, and statutory authorities.

- AISs are designed for accounting functions. In financial accounting functions, an AIS is designed for and complies with the Generally Accepted Accounting Principles (GAAP), International Financial Reporting Standards (IFRS), International Accounting Standards Board (IASB), and relevant local and international standards to produce relevant financial statements. Three key components of financial statements are cash flow, profit and loss, and financial position, which can all be produced by AISs.

- AISs produce financial reports based on historical data and internal sources (business transactions). Financial information and statements can be used for various purposes.

- The financial information produced by the AISs should be identical to that produced by the manual approach. The optimal goals of the AIS are to provide efficiency and effective operations and to produce error-free financial statements and reports. The financial statements are used by external and internal users.

- AISs provide greater security management and controls. With appropriately deployed security and defense strategies, they can reduce faults and crime. However, this also introduces a need for cyber security and management.

- AISs can provide backups of master files to maintain a higher level of data integrity and security.

Characteristics of Accounting Information
Accounting information can be characterized as relevant, reliable, complete, timely, understandable, verifiable, and accessible (Collier, 20015; Romney and Steinbart, 2016; Fang and Shu, 2016).

- Accessible—information must be available and obtainable.
- Complete—information must be sufficient to allow users to make decisions.
- Relevant—information can be used to help make decisions.
- Reliable—information must be free of errors and bias.
- Timing—information timing is critical to making decisions.
- Understandable—information must be presented in a way that users can easily interpret.
- Verifiable—information must be consistently traceable with errors and bias.

There are several advantages of AISs, including improving the quality of information and reducing human errors for large transactions. It also can reduce long-term costs, particularly with a high volume of transactions and operational costs. AISs can significantly improve internal controls by reducing human risk, particularly when organizations deal with financial data (Collier, 2015). Overall, AISs can produce timely and accurate data on which users can base decisions.

Chapter 2

Accounting Cycle and System Architecture

Accounting Cycle and Process

The key to an accounting cycle is to capture relevant financial data for accounting reporting under Generally Accepted Accounting Principles (GAAP) (Fawcett and Martin, 2016; Collier, 2015). The GAAP is a set of accounting standards and procedures with which the companies must compile their reporting financial statements. Two main accounting transaction cycles are revenue and expenditure (see Figure 1). Figure 1 shows an example of sales processes in the revenue cycle: a company receives a sale order, ships goods/services, bills the customer, and receives payment. The purchase processes include a company making a purchase order to a supplier for goods/services, receiving the goods/services, recording in an account payable, and paying the supplier. There is a set of sequential and interrelated activities in both revenue and expenditure cycles.

Figure 1: Revenue and Purchase Cycles.

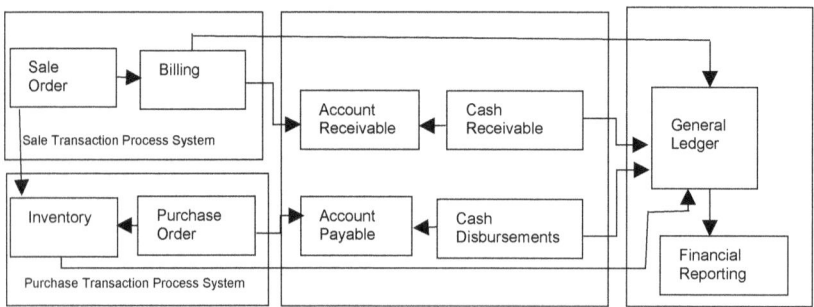

Basic Accounting Information System Architecture

The traditional view of the AIS focuses on the input-process-output model (see Figure 2) (Ward and Peppard, 2016; Pearlson et al., 2016). The AIS in day-to-day transactions and operations refers to transaction processing systems (TPS). The TPS, for example, is a point-of-sale system that generates sale transactions. Management information systems summarize and aggregate the primary data. The outputs refer to relevant reports, such as financial, scheduled, and ad hoc reports for end users.

Figure 2: Basic Accounting Information System Input-Process-Output Model.

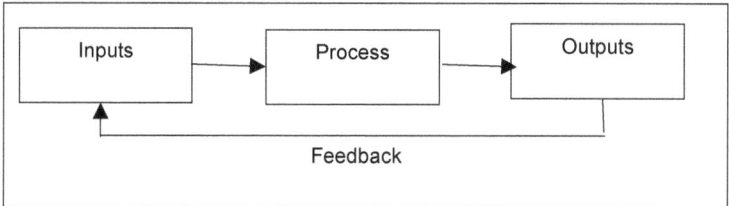

An AIS architecture is a formal documentation and representation of a system that makes use of elements of hardware and software. It is a conceptual model. This model provides information about the structure and behavior of the system. Figure 3 shows a simple system architecture. The model shows that each computer or process on the network is either a client or server (also known as client-server architecture). The clients are the end-user's computers, and servers are the service providers. The servers are generally more powerful computers and distributed applications that provide different tasks and functions, such as file servers (managing disk drives), network servers (network traffic), and data warehouse (multiple database servers) (Pearlson et al., 2016; Kataria et al., 2016; Pathan, 2011).

Figure 3: Accounting Information Systems Client Server Architecture.

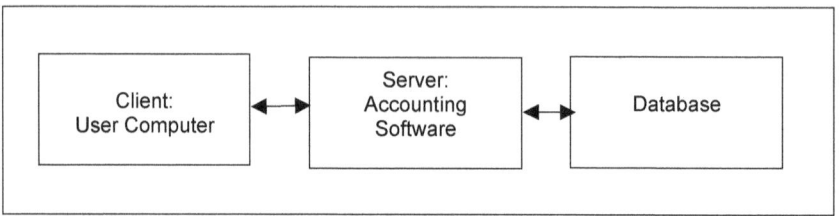

Cloud Computing Architecture

Cloud computing is an internet-based computing that provides shared computer processing resources and data storage to computers and other devices (Pearlson et al., 2016). The shared-configuration computer resources include networks, services, data storage, software, applications, and servers (Chidambaram et al., 2016). Many cloud computing service providers offer one-stop services. The main reasons are due to low costs of services, high demand of computing power, high performance, scalability, accessibility, and availability. Figure 4 shows the cloud computing architecture, where the end users can access the system via network servers/devices (e.g., router and switch).

Figure 4: Cloud Computing Architecture.

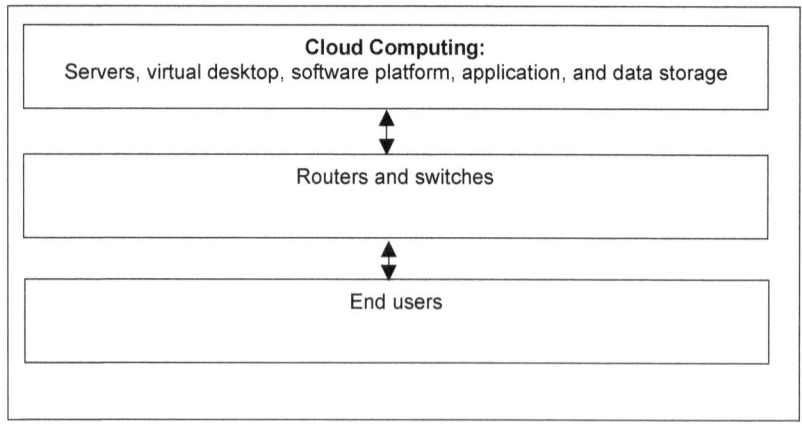

Digital Architecture
With the fast growth of internet business and social media technology in cloud computing, more customer-focused digital architecture is developed, in addition to the integration of digital platform and external integration (i.e., social media clouds) (Napoli et al., 2016). A new trend of the digital architecture focuses on active engagement of customers and stakeholders (Ward and Peppard, 2016). It uses the external cloud infrastructure, such as public, partner, and social clouds, as well as external applications, devices, and data. The key benefits of deploying digital architecture are (Chidambaram et al., 2016; Napoli et al., 2016; Ward and Peppard, 2016):

- Creating value chain in business process.
- Allowing the company to actively engage its customers and stakeholders.
- Integrating social media and external cloud platforms.
- Integrating mobile and wireless devices.
- Providing three different views that include users, marketing and sales, and technology.
- Providing better user experiences.

Chapter 3

Cyber Security

What is Cyber Security?
Cyber security is often associated with information technology security (Kim and Solomon, 2013). In information technology security, the general concerns are for internal and external controls of computer hardware, software, networks, and databases. The overall goal is to protect valuable information technology assets and reduce all possible risks (Choucri et al., 2016). The term "cyber security" is interchangeable with "information technology security". With fast growth in internet and wireless technologies, as well as increases in the number of mobile and wireless devices, the needs to address possible vulnerabilities are highly prioritized by many governments and companies (Gupta, 2016). In addition, the value of financial data in an Accounting Information System is a critical element. Thus, cyber security has become a topic of growing importance in accounting information systems.

Vulnerability
A vulnerability refers to an information system susceptibility. Cybercrime is a serious concern in cybersecurity. Common defenses for vulnerabilities include security by design, network security, infrastructure security, hardware security, system security, human security, auditing, testing, and making changes (McDowell, 2015; Raggad, 2010; Gupta 2016).

Cybercrime
Cybercrime is one of the major concerns around the world. Earth currently has a population of approximately 7.4 billion; approximately 3.5 billion of these are internet users, and 6.5 billion phones are connected worldwide (Worldometers, 2016; Wikipedia, 2016). The risk of fraud, theft, abuse, and harassment has greatly increased. Therefore, it is necessary to prioritize cyber-criminal investigations and to defeat and protect network security. An

example of cybercrime includes sending fake CEO emails to an accounting and finance department; the FBI reported cybercrimes cost US businesses more than $2 billion in just two years (Scannell, 2016).

Security by Design
To design a secure system, the architecture of the system must address risks that apply control strategies to a specific domain area and/or environment. The key attributes of security architecture are: (a) determination of controls based on best practices, as well as financial and regulation requirements; and (b) the interdependency of the system components (Rakitin, 2016). When designing a security system, the security attributes are confidentiality, integrity, availability, and accountability.

In software development, software can be focused on security features. There are a few approaches in creating security by design (Kim and Solomon, 2016; Wong, 2006).

- Software review—software review is one of the most common approaches to ensure quality of software, and to produce software that is free of errors (Wong, 2006). In software review, developers inspect the software to ensure it meets the security requirements. This can occur in any phase of software development.
- Software testing—software testing is usually conducted in the later phase of the system implementation. This allows testers to conduct final testing against the requirements (Wong, 2003).
- Principle of least privilege—designing software with limited access or with some parts of the system being restricted to certain users. This can reduce the impact of attackers who gain access to the system.
- Defense in-depth—also refers to the Castle approach. In information assurance, multiple layers of security controls can be implemented in information technology. The security controls should be included in all aspects of

technical, physical and procedural, during the system development.

- Audit trails—audit logs, trails, and tracking systems identify security breaches and the attacker's activity history. An instruction detection system analyses the attacker's behavior and the vulnerability of the system.
- Automated theorem proving (also known as automated deduction)—using automated reasoning or mathematical logic for dealing with mathematical theorems. Commercial uses of automated theorem proving are mainly focused on verification and/or integrated circuit design. For an example, Intel uses automated theorem proving to verify the correctness of its processers' operations.
- Security by default—refers to the 'secure configuration setting', which is the most secure setting. However, users can change the user-friendly preference setting. Software generally runs both risk analysis and usability tests. In a network operation system, there are no open network ports (i.e. no listening INET domain sockets after installation). This can be checked and verified by a local machine, such as a port scanner. Abstraction is another approach to securing the software in such a manner that no data loss can be caused by user mistake or accident.
- Full disclosure—refers to the publishing of all security attacks so that the information is accessible to everyone. The practice of making the public aware of the vulnerabilities as early as possible aims to reduce the duration of a vulnerability from when a security beach is first identified to as short as possible.

Infrastructure Security

Infrastructure vulnerabilities include three major areas: physical, database, and operations (Edwards et al., 2016; Jamei et al., 2016; Bhardwaj et al., 2016). Physical security refers to the foundation of security infrastructure. To protect all physical elements, a common security setup uses surveillance systems with security personnel, access control/instruction detection systems, and recording cameras to ensure a high level of physical infrastructure security. Managing a database considers three factors: multiple levels of access using multiple carrier-grade access routers, distributions, switches, and POD switches to ensure no single point of failure. Power control, environment control (e.g., temperature and humidity), and back up in different locations (e.g., multiple sites) help ensure that no disaster can affect the infrastructure. An operation support team can also provide monitoring of technical and non-technical issues related to the infrastructure (Martinez et al., 2013). Operation support teams provide internal auditing, incident support, and review tools for continual management (Wong, 2009). In operation security, a separation of duty models can be enforced by implementing access control lists and capability-based security. The access control list is a table or a list that provides permission for each user to access a system object. Capability-based security refers to the principle of least privilege, in which users can share capabilities with each other. The benefit of the capability-based security in system infrastructure is that it helps provide efficient and secure transactions.

Network Security

Network security consists of policies, techniques, and tools such as defense-in-depth design, adopted to prevent unauthorized access, misuse, modification, or interruptions in an authorized user's access to a computer network and accessible resources (Martinez et al., 2014; Gupta et al., 2016). The vulnerabilities of a network result from data access authorization, and are normally managed by network administrators. Generally, firewalls enforce network security policies for access control. Identity checks that determine the username and password are undertaken in order to authenticate a user; this is often referred to as one-factor authentication. Many financial entities use two-factor authentication such as ATM cards, mobile phones, and security tokens. Additional security authentication uses biometric techniques such as fingerprint scans. Cryptographic techniques are also used for encryption and decryption for protecting data and information resources (Gupta, 2016). Common potential risks for network security are computer worms and Trojans. Preventive security software and tools often used for these are anti-virus software, intrusion prevention systems, and anti-malware software. Network communication is encrypted to maintain privacy and security. Network security policies may also use an intrusion detection system to monitor the network and traffic with logs and audit trials. Honeypots are often employed for the analysis of an attacker's behavior and activities, also referred to as exploitation. This allows the network administrator to review current security policies and provide further advancement for the prevention of future cyber-attacks.

Network security design is one of the most crucial areas in cyber security and includes firewall sections, engagement addresses, network segmentation, access control policies, and technology selections to accommodate a company's needs (Pathan, 2011). The design of a network architecture can be considered across multiple areas, including anti-virus protection, directory services, instruction detection systems (IDSs), business continuity, perimeter defense, routers, secure AID, virtual private networks (VPN), wireless network remote access, secure e-commerce, enterprise backup, and firewalls (Pathan, 2011).

System Security

Security systems have multiple controls, including physical controls and vulnerability scans, to identify system vulnerabilities. They may also include photo identity, entrance and access points verification, security personnel, physical cameras, video recording, and power backup to ensure a high level of physical control. Vulnerability scans routinely scan and monitor all activities to identify possible vulnerabilities and reinforce security policies.

Hardware Security

Common hardware security techniques and devices include trusted platform modules, drive locks, dongles, disabling USB ports, biometric readers, and Roots of Trust in mobile hardware security (Martinez et al., 2014; Pathan, 2011; Shim et al., 2013).

- Trusted platform modules are secure devices built into the RSA cryptographic keys (endorsement keys) for hardware authentication (Rostami et al., 2013). In conjunction with the host server, the trust platform module chips (computer-on-chips) are used for preventing unauthorized network and data access.
- Drive lock software tools can be used to encrypt hard drives and to ensure they are inaccessible to thieves (Shim et al., 2013).
- Dongles are small devices that use the Advanced Encryption Standard for providing a strong measure of security. Dongles have multiple functions. They can be used with computers for protecting and authorizing access to computers and software. They also provide access controls to wireless broadband. Another feature of dongles is that they can be configured to lock or unlock computers and software.
- A disabled USB port is a hardware security tool that prevents users from connecting to a USB storage device or malicious attack. The disabled USB port can help isolate the network to keep it from becoming infected with malware or other viruses. It can be especially useful to prevent unauthorized access to data.
- Biometric verification and validation, such as fingerprint readers, QR code readers, and voice recognitions can be

implemented in computer hardware or access control points (Wong et al., 2005).

- Roots of Trust (RoTs) in mobile hardware security are the foundation of assurance of trustworthiness of a mobile device. Hardware RoTs provide more assurance of support device integrity, isolation, verification, and storage protection (Rasquier et al., 2015).

Human Security

Human security ensures all data is protected with security controls to avoid risks (Solms and NieKerk, 2013). One of the critical elements is to hire quality personnel who have no criminal record and are trustworthy (Wong, 2009). This can be done by conducting criminal database checks and background screens to ensure all employees are appropriately appointed. By developing security awareness and education, users will have a better understanding of information technology security and cyber security (Raggad, 2010). The overall objective of human security is to develop a security culture in which each user can recognize security risks, take responsibility, and be accountable for the security.

Auditing, Testing, and Making Changes

To achieve zero risk or to minimize possible vulnerabilities, the important elements are (McDowell, 2015; Raggad, 2010; Wang et al., 2013):

1 Define security policy.
2 Assess compliance.
3 Monitor policy violations.
4 Routinely test for and minimize exposure to risks.
5 Routinely review all identified threats.

Upon completion of auditing and testing (e.g., external security auditors can perform penetration tests), implementing change controls is the final step in developing a robust infrastructure. The change control can establish appropriate authorization for requesting, designing, implementing, testing, and validating all changes. In accounting practices, it is critical to ensure that a zero-risk level can be achieved.

Chapter 4

Cyber-attacks, Controls, and Defenses

There have been a range of cyber-attacks in the past two decades. Common cyber-attacks include backdoors, clickjacking, denial-of-service attacks, direct access attacks, eavesdropping, malvertising, phishing, and tampering.

Backdoor

Backdoor refers to the access of a computer program that bypasses security mechanisms. This is often a remote access and a targeted attack. In most cases, hackers take advantage of a backdoor to access a victim's infrastructure without being detected. Common backdoor attacks include (Bailey et al., 2005; Sushama et al., 2016; Gaffney, 2013; Klick et al., 2015):

- Port binding (utilized before firewalls are in place).
- Connect-back (hackers leverage a backdoor to connect the targeted systems).
- Connect availability use (use of malware).
- Legitimate platform abuse (attack a valid weak system, such as blog).
- Secret method to bypass authentication (adding an authorized party for legitimate access).

Controls and Defenses:

1. Use firewalls in all entry points to block all unauthorized users.
2. Use a robust network detection system to monitor a network, particularly in an open source program (Martinez et al., 2014).
3. Implement anti-malware software.

Clickjacking

Clickjacking is another common attack that is a malicious technique to trick a user into clicking on a button or link on another webpage

(Huang et al., 2012; Nagarhalli et al., 2016). The attack often uses the "bait-and-switch" approach to trick users; when clicking buttons or links, the user is switched to another website or to something else. Clickjacking is also known as User Interface (UI) redress attack.

Controls and defenses:

1. User confirmation can set a requirement to reconfirm the information.
2. UI randomization randomizes the UI position to prevent attackers from finding and locating the targeted position (Nagarhalli et al., 2016).
3. Frame-busting (x-frame-option) is used to prevent a site from functioning when loaded inside a frame (Kavitha et al., 2016).
4. Opaque overlay policy (Gazelle browser) is used to provide a transparency of the website (Kavitha et al., 2016).
5. Visibility detection on click (no script); a site provides a detection that does not allow scripts; for example, the Firefox browser has implemented visibility detection techniques (Shahriar and Haddad, 2015; Pawade et al., 2016).
6. Imposing delay techniques so that users think before clicking on buttons or links. Usually, users need to wait for a few seconds before they can click (Moshchuk et al., 2012).
7. Dynamic OS-level screenshot comparison to ensure integrity of the target click, and that it is an exact match with the same image of pixels (Huang et al, 2012).
8. Freeze screen around the target that allows users to stop clicking on the fake link or button (Huang et al, 2012).
9. Pointer re-entry technique that, after visual changes on the target, invalidates the click until pointer re-entry (AlJarrah and Shehab, 2016). That means the user's first click is invalidated, and a re-click would be validated.

Denial-of-service

Denial-of-service attacks aim to make the network resources unavailable to users (Ali et al., 2015). Attackers aim to interrupt the services from a host connected to the internet. Distributed denial-of-service (DDoS) refers to multiple points of attack; i.e., more than one–or thousands–of unique IP addresses attack multiple hosts or networks. Examples of denial-of-service attacks include (1) attackers deliberately entering the wrong password consecutive times to lock out users, (2) overloading the network to block out multiple users at once, (3) zombies (botnets) attacking with forwarding transmissions (including spam or viruses) to other computers on the internet, (4) a misconfigured Domain Name System (DNS) server can be easily exploited in an amplification attack in which an attacker tries to overwhelm a victim system with DNS response traffic (Booth and Anderson, 2015; Chouhan and Singh, 2016).

Controls and defenses:

1. Application front-end hardware is used to analyze data packets' priority, and determine whether it is regular and/or dangerous (Chouhan and Singh, 2016). This is a front-end hardware that can be installed on the network, such as on routers and switches, before traffic reaches the servers (Rouvinen, 2015).
2. Key completion indicators (KCIs) are designed in cloud-based applications to fight against DDoS attacks in cloud computing (Khan et al., 2016). The KCIs use a probabilistic approach to analyze legitimate incoming traffic before deploying elasticity policies (Jing et al., 2015).
3. Black hole is one of the common methods used against DoS or DDoS attacks (Tyagi, 2016). In networking or network topology, black hole refers to incoming or outgoing traffic that is silently discarded without approaching a receiver. In internet management, a DNS Blackhole List (DNSBL), also known as a blacklist, blocklist, or a Real-time Blackhole List (RBL), is often used in conjunction with mail server and spam software to analyze traffic and remove attacks silently (Tyagi, 2016). Black hole email addresses can be removed silently without users' awareness. In internet TPC/IP protocols, all IP addresses require communication with host machines. When there is failure in communication with the host machines, the IP address will be automatically discarded before approaching the receiver.

4. An Intrusion Prevention System (IPS) examines network traffic, detects malicious activities or violations, and prevents vulnerability exploits (Yan et al., 2016). The IPS provides alarms to the network administrator, delivers malicious packets, blocks traffic from the source address, and resets the connection. Two main types of IPSs include network-based IPSs (NIPS) and host-based IPSs (HIPS) (Khan, 2016; Prabha and Sree, 2016). The NIPS are deployed as webservers right in front of the critical resources, whereas the HIPS are set up inside a host system, which only protects the host itself. IPSs were popular mid-2000. Nowadays, IPSs are integrated into firewalls, intrusion detection systems, and unified threat management solutions (Prabha and Sree, 2016).

5. Firewall rules based on ports, IP addresses, and protocols can be deployed for a simple attack. For more complex attacks, Next Generation FireWall (NGFW) appliances combine with network firewalls and IPSs to provide better malware protection (Keskin et al., 2016).

6. Denial-of-service defense systems (DDSs) address IPS limitations that can block connection-based attacks, such as DDSs defense protocol attacks. The protocol attack refers to exploiting specific features or implementing bugs in some of the victim's protocols to consume an excessive amount of resources. Examples of protocol attacks include Smurf, SYN, ICMP, CGI requests, authentication server, attacks using DNS systems, and attacks using spoofed addresses in ping (Singh and Panda, 2015).

7. Routers and switches both have a rate-limiting approach, and they can be used to access control models to build access controls and capability lists. These can reduce the impact of traffic flooding resulting from the DoS attacks. Some switches can perform automatic filtering, traffic shaping, delayed binding, deep packet inspection, and Bogon-Filtering to detect DoS attacks.

8. Ingress filtering is a technique to counter against DoS and spoofing attacks (Ayyaz et al., 2016). It identifies fake IP addresses and verifies incoming packets from the originate networks.

9. Network administrators can use Unicast Reverse Path Forwarding (URPF) to limit the flow of malicious attacks on the network, such as DoS attacks. URPF checks the source of IP addresses that match the correct source of the interface according to the routing table.
10. Geographic dispersion (Global Resources Any-cast) is a newer technique against DDoS attacks that distributes footprints of DDoS attacks (Berman et al., 2016). By using the Any-cast routing method, traffic from a source is allowed to be routed to various nodes of networks. Global resource Any-cast is one of several effective countermeasures to DDoS attacks, as it can find nearby Any-cast resources topologically closest to itself. Any-cast architecture can improve internet presence security and reliability.
11. DoS run book provides a playbook or manual for a company in the event a DoS attack arises. This run book provides a crisis management and plan to deal with network environment, including rules, recovery, and solution mitigation plans (Silva et al., 2017).
12. A filtering list (reputation-based blocking) is a critical component in today's cyber security (Don et al., 2016). Reputation-based techniques provide URL analysis and identify threat telemetry, intelligence engineers, and analytics. The aim is to establish a reputation for each URL. It also blocks or limits the impact of untrustworthy URLs.
13. Connection limits and timeouts can be used for DoS defense purposes. They are a common feature in a network environment, used to ensure that DoS attacks are unable to enter the inside zones of an internal network. They use connection limits and timeouts.

Direct Access
A direct access attack is unauthorized physical access of a computer. Attacks include operating system modifications, installing malicious devices, software viruses and worms, key loggers, and wireless mice.

Controls and defenses:

1. Encrypt and backup all valuable data.
2. Deploy separate storage servers.

Eavesdropping

Eavesdropping is secretly listening to private conversations of others without their consent. The eavesdropping attack can occur in different forms of communication, such as email, online chatroom, and Voice Over Internet Protocol (VOIP). A network eavesdropping attack can be done over a network layer; attackers capture packets during the transmission when the network lacks an encryption service (Zou and Wang, 2016; He et al., 2014).

Controls and defenses:

1. SSL (secure sockets layer) protocol can encrypt online communication and secure data over the internet (Huang et al., 2014). An SSL certificate is one of the solutions to secure servers and websites. The SSL is a protocol for transmission technology for encrypted links or private documents between a client and a sever, such as a web server and a browser or a mail server. In the cryptographic system, a public key (everyone) and a private key (only the recipient) are used in the SSL design. Encryption with the SSL certificate helps to protect data from being stolen or sniffed.
2. Public Key Infrastructure (PKI) is designed to secure sensitive information such as e-commerce and e-banking over the internet (He et al., 2014). The PKI is a set of policies and procedures that is designed to verify digital certificates, provide server authentication, and manage public key encryption.
3. Antivirus and malware scan software can be set up to alert a user about any malicious attack or virus, as well as to keep most viruses out of the system.
4. Firewalls are a common technique to project network traffics for any malicious attack or unauthorized access.

5. Network intrusion prevention systems detect and avert eavesdroppers.
6. Network segmentation refers to a computer network that is divided or split into sub-networks that can restrict unauthorized traffic (Du et al., 2014). It also improves network performance and security.
7. Network Access Controls (NAC) is an endpoint security server (or technology) that enforces trustworthy systems and network authentication (Yue et al., 2013). In addition, NAC can restrict data access to different individual users.
8. Password security is also important in security attacks. Frequently change passwords to a strong, long password that includes a combination of small and capital alphabets with letters, numbers, and special characters.

Malvertising

Malvertising is similar to clickjacking. A malvertising attack is based on end users clicking on a web advertisement (Xing et al., 2015). The computer then downloads malicious code onto the user's system.

Controls and defenses:

1. Many ads, such as free software downloads or free trips, are too good to be true. They allow malware to be easily downloaded onto your system.
2. Up-to-date software and operating systems can reduce the risks of an attack.
3. User training and education ensures the best knowledge of cyber-attacks and how to avoid them and defend against them.

Phishing

According to the Phishing Trends and Intelligence Report in 2016, there are more than one million confirmed malicious phishing sites on over 130,000 unique domains (PhishLabs, 2016).

The main goal of phishing is to steal sensitive information, such as financial and personal information, credit card details, passwords, and usernames (Amiri et al., 2014). Phishing attackers focus on manipulating users' trust, and most phishing techniques are carried out by email spoofing and instant messaging. In e-commerce, many fake websites aim to target victims' personal and/or financial details. Malware is one of the most commonly used phishing attacks. Attackers use malicious code with an intent to steal data and destroy a computer.

Controls and defenses:

1. User training is one of the most critical defenses against the attacks. Best practices and up-to-date security training can significantly reduce the cybercrime and related financial risks.
2. SSL certificate security and two-factor authentication communication can be set up to reduce the risk of phishing attacks (Bicakci et al., 2014).
3. Anti-virus, internet scanner, and spam software provide filtering and detect any phishing email messages, websites, and links.
4. Use the latest security updates in an operating system.

Privilege Escalation
Privilege escalation attackers take the weakness of a poor operating system and software configurations, design flaws, and bugs in order to gain access to restricted system areas (Heuser et al., 2016).

Controls and defenses:

1. Remove the complier, as many AIS do not need it. Attackers often require the complier to develop an exploit. This can significantly reduce the risk of attacks.
2. File integrity monitoring (FIM) software uses verification methods as a baseline that validates the integrity of application software and file, and operates the system (Gupta et al., 2015). The verification method often makes a

comparison of cryptographic checksums between the original baseline and the current state of files. These verification methods can be done in automation real-time, randomly, and polling interval for internal control.

3. Advanced Intrusion Detection Environment (AIDE) is also used for integrity tests and for building a database that can be stored in external devices (Kenkre et al., 2014). It can be used to make a comparison between the previously built database and the current status of the system.

4. System audits (e.g. Lynis) and tools (e.g., Linux Enumeration (LinEnum) & Unix-privesc-checker) can perform security audits and detect risks in the operating system (Manu et al., 2016).

5. Patch systems apply regular updates for interactive login privileges and use content registry for tracking.

Spoofing

Spoofing is a network malicious attack where an unknown source is sent to the receiver to gain illegitimate benefits (Fan et al., 2015; Psiaki et al., 2016; Sathya et al., 2016). Common attacks include caller ID spoofing (e.g., false ID and number in VoIP), email spoofing (e.g., spammers hide the origin of their emails), man-in-the-middle attacks (e.g., TPC/IP internet protocol does not provide mechanisms for authenticating the source), and referrer header spoofing (e.g., users gain unauthorized access due to incorrect sending of referrer in HTTP network requests for websites) (Gupta and Gola, 2016; Mahadev et al., 2016).

Controls and defenses:

1. In software development, spoofing often can be tested by penetration testing for observing the HTTP Daemon (HTTPD) system. The HTTPD is a software program that runs in the background of a web server and automatically responds to all web requests.

2. Proxy servers and some software tools are already installed in web browsers (e.g., Internet Explorer and Mozilla Firefox) that can manage referrer URLs and HTTP requests.

3. Cross-Site Request Forgery (CSRF) prevention techniques can be used by embedding additional authentication access controls, such as additional data requests to detect any unauthorized location (Gupta and Gola, 2016).
4. A detection system can be installed for monitoring the address resolution protocol (ARP) table, detecting changes of gateway entry (e.g., comparing outputs with previous saved IP/Mac entry) and alerting the victim.
5. In mobile or caller ID spoofing, the call-back method or search engine can be used to verify the information.
6. The Completely Automated Public Turing test to tell Computers and Human Apart (CAPTCHA) can be used to determine whether the attacker is human (Mahadev et al., 2016).
7. Personal safety techniques, such as avoiding saving usernames and passwords in a browser, logging off immediately after using a web application, using different browsers for accessing sensitive information, and using plugins (e.g., no script) to reduce attacks, particularly in JavaScript.

Tampering

Tampering refers to an attack without authority that causes damage to a victim. This involves altering or modifying information, a product, or a system. Web parameter tampering attacks involve the manipulation of parameter transmission between client and server and the altering of information. Paros proxy and Web-Scarab are the common security tools.

Consequence attacks such as cross-site scripting (XSS), path traversal, and SQL injection can be exploited due to errors of integrity and logic validation mechanism (Selim et al., 2016). XSS aims to inject client-side scripts viewing a user's side websites. A path traversal is also known as directory traversal, directory climbing, backtracking, or dot-dot-slash, and is an attempt to gain access to files or a directory. SQL injection is the insertion of a SQL query including reading, executing database administrative operation, and storing data contents.

Controls and defenses:

1. Training and educating users about tampering attacks and defenses.
2. User Behavior Analytics (UBA) review human behavior by applying algorithms and statistical analysis to detect meaningful anomalies (Shen et al., 2016).
3. Multiple access controls and limited access policies for different users.

References

Ali M., Khan S.U. and Vasilako A.V. (2015). Security in Cloud Computing: Opportunities and Challenges. Information Sciences, Elsevier, vol.305, pp.357-383.

AlJarrah A. and Shehab M. (2016). Maintaining User Interface Integrity on Android. Proceedings of IEEE 40th Annual Computer Software and Applications (COMPASC'16), 10-14 June. Atlanta, Georgia.

Amiri I.S., Akanbi O.A. and Fazeldehkordi E. (2015). A Machine-Learning Approach to Phishing Detection and Defense. Waltham: Elsevier.

Ayyaz S., Khan M.A., Ahmad J., Beard C., Choi B.Y. and Saqib N.A. (2016). A Novel Security System for Preventing DoS Attacks on 4C LTE Networks, Proceedings of International Conference on Wireless Network ICWN'16. 25-28 July, Las Vega, Nevada.

Bailey M., Cook E., Jahanian F., Nazario J. and Waston D. (2005). The Internet Motion Sensor-A Distributed Blackhole Monitoring System. NDSS.

Berman K., Demeester P., Lee J.W., Nagaraja K., Zink M., Colle D., Kumar D., Raychaudhuri D., Schulzinne H., Seskar I. and Sharma S. (2016). Future Internet Scape the Simulator. Communications of ACM. 58(6), pp.78-89.

Bhardwaj A., Subrahmanyam G.V.G., Avasthi V. and Sastry H. (2016). Design a Resilient Network Infrastructure Security Policy Framework. Indian Journal of Science and Technology, 9(19), pp.1-8.

Bicakci K., Unal D. and Ascioglu N. (2014). Mobile Authentication Secure Against Man-in-the-Middle Attacks. Proceedings of 2nd IEEE International Conference on Mobile Cloud Computing, Services, and Engineering, MobileCloud'2014. 7-10 April. Oxford, UK.

Booth T.G. and Andersson K. (2015). Elimination of DoS UDP Reflection Amplification Bandwidth Attacks, Protecting TCP Services, Proceedings of International Conference on Future Network Systems: Communications in Computer and Information Science, 11-13 June, vol.512, pp.1-15. Paris, France.

Chidambaram N., Raj P., Thenmozhi K., and Amirtharajan R. (2016). Enhancing the Security of Customer Data in Cloud Environments Using a Novel Digital Fingerprinting Technique. International Journal of Digital Multimedia Broadcasting.

Choucri M., Madnick S. and Koepke P. (2016) Institutions for Cyber Security: International Responses and Data Sharing Initiatives. Aug, Working paper, CISL No.2016-10

Chouhan P. and Singh R. (2016). Security Attacks on Cloud Computing with Possible Solution. International Journal of Advanced Research in Computer Sciences and Software Engineering. 6(1), pp.93-96.

Collier P.M. (2015). Accounting for managers: Interpreting Accounting Information for Decision Making, Wiley Publisher.

Edwards N., Kao G., Hamlet J., Bailon J. and Liptak S. (2016). Supply Chain Decision Analytics: Application and Case Study for Critical Infrastructure Security. Proceedings of 11th International Conference on Cyber Warfare and Security. 17-18 March. Boston: Boston University.

Don E., Gupta N., Landberg F. and Sturges J. (2016). System, Apparatus, and Method for Protecting a Network Using Internet Protocol Reputation Information. US Patent: 9319382B2.

Du R., Zhao C., Li S. and Li J. (2014). Efficient Weakly Secure Network Coding Scheme Against Node Conspiracy Attack Based on Network Segmentation. Journal on Wireless Communications and Networking. Springer Link.

Fan Y., Zhang Z. and Trinkle M. (2015). Cross-Layer Defense Mechanism Against GPS Spoofing Attacks on PMUs in Smart Grids. IEEE Transaction on Smart Grid. 6(6), pp.2659-2668.

Fang J. and Shu L. (2016). Modern Accounting Information System Security (AISS) Research Based on IT Technology. Advanced Science and Technology Letters (AST 2016). vol.121, pp.163-170.

Fawcett M. and Martin D. (2016). Accounting Information Systems. Forest Lodge: Better Teams Publications.

Gaffney T. (2013). Following in the Footsteps of Window: How Android Malware Development Is Looking Very Familiar, Journal of Network Security. 8, pp.7-10. Elsevier.

Gupta J. and Gola (2016) Server Side Protection Against Cross Site Request Forgery Using CSFR Gateway, Journal of Information Technology and Software. 6:128

Gupta J. (2016) Handbook of Research on Modern Cryptographic Solutions for Computer and Cyber Security, p.317, IGI.

Gupta S., Kumar P., and Abraham A. (2015) A Resource-Efficient Integrity Monitoring and Response Approach for Cloud Computing Environment. Advances in Intelligent Systems and Computing, vol.355, pp.335-349.

He D., Chan S., Zhang Y., Guizani M. and Chen C. (2014) An Enhanced Public Key Infrastructure to Secure Smart Grid Wireless Communication Networks, IEEE Networks, 28(1), 10-16.

Heuser S., Negro M., Pendyala P.K. and Sadeghi A.R. (2016) DroidAuditor: Forensic Analysis of Application-Layer Privilege Escalation Attacks on Android, CASED, Technical Report: r.tud-cs-2016-0025.

Huang L.S., Moshchuk A., Wang H.J. and Stuart S. (2012) Clickjacking: Attacks and Defenses, Proceedings of The 21st Usenix Security Symposium, 8-10 Aug. Bellevue: The Advanced Computing Systems Association.

Huang L.S., Rice A. and Ellingsen E. (2014). Analyzing Forged SSL Certificates in the Wild, Proceedings of 2014 IEEE Symposium on Security and Privacy (SP'14). 18-21 May. San Jose, CA.

Jamei M., Emma S., Scaglione A. and Ciaran R. (2016). Micro Synchrophasor-Based Instruction Detection in Automated Distribution Systems: Toward Critical Infrastructure Security, IEEE Internet Computing, 20(5), pp.18-27.

Jing X., Bai D., Feng F., Chen L. and Zho Y. (2015). Detection for Application-Layer Denial of Service Attack Based on Cluster Analysis. Proceedings of Information Science and Cloud Computing (ISCC'15). 18-19 Dec. Guangzhou, China.

Kataria M., Leland M.G. and Presler-Marshall M.J.C. (2016). Adaptable Application in a Client/ Server Architecture. US Patent No: 9443213.

Kavitha D., Chandrasekaran S. and Rani S.K. (2016). HDTCV: Hybrid Detection Techniques for Clickjacking Vulnerability, Artificial Intelligence and Evolutionary Computation Engineering Systems: Advances in Intelligent Systems and Computing. vol.394. pp.607-620, Springer.

Kenkre P.S., Pai A. and Colaco L. (2014). Real Time Intrusion Detection and Prevention System, Proceedings of the 3rd International Conference on Frontiers of Intelligent Computing: Theory and Applications (FICTA'14). vol.327, pp.405-411.

Kim D. and Solomon M.G. (2013). Fundamentals of Information Systems Security, 2nd Edition, Burlington: Jones and Bartletts Learning.

Klick J., Lau D., and Marzin D. and Malchow J.O. (2015). Internet-Facing PLCs As a Network Backdoor, Proceedings of IEEE Conference on Communications, and Network Security (CNS), 28-30 Sept. Florence, Italy.

Khan, M.A. (2016). A Survey of Security Issues for Could Computing, Journal of Network and Computer Applications, Elsevier, 71, pp.11-29.

Mahadve, Kumar V. and Kumar K. (2016). Classification of DDoS Attack Tools and its Handling Techniques and Strategy at Application Layer. Proceedings of International Conference on Advances in Communication and Automation. 30 Sep-1 Oct.

Manu A.R., Patel J.K. and Akhtar S. (2016). A Study, Analysis and Deep Dive on Cloud PAAS Security in Terms of Docker Container Security, Proceedings of International Conference on Circuit, Power and Computing Technologies (ICCPCT'16). 18-19 March.

Martinez A., Yannuzzi M. and Lopez V. (2014). Network Management Challenges and Trends in Multi-Layer and Multi-Vendor Settings for Carrier-Grade Networks. IEEE Communications Surveys & Tutorials. 16(4). 2207 - 2230

Mayberry M. D. (2013). CAATTs Ideal for Efficient Audits. American Institute of CPAs (accessed 6 Jan 2016).

McDowell, G. L. (2015). Cracking the Code Interview: 189 Programming Questions and Solutions. 6th Edition.

Moshchuk A.N., Wang J.H. and Schechter S. (2012). Defending Against Clicking Attacks. US Patent: 20140155701A1.

Nagarhalli T.P., Bakal J.W. and Jain N. (2016). A Brief Survey of Detection and Mitigation Techniques for Clickjacking and Drive-by Download Attack. International Journal of Computer Applications. 138(2). pp.44-48.

Napoli C., Pappalardo G., Tramontana E. and Zappala G. (2016). A Cloud-distributed GPU Architecture for Pattern Identification in Segmented Defectors Big-Data Surveys. The Computer Journal. 59(3). pp.338-325.

Pasquier T.F.J.M, Singh J., Bacon J. (2015). Cloud of Things Need Information Flow Control with Hardware Roots of Trust. 2015 IEEE 7th International Conference on Cloud Computing Technology and Science (CloudCom). 30Nov-3Dec. Vancouver, BC, Canada.

Pathan A.S.K. (2011). Security of Self-Organizing Networks: MANET, WSN, WMN, VANET, Boca Raton: CRC Press, Taylor & Francis Group

Pawade D., Reji D., and Lahigude A. (2016). Implementation of Extension for Browser to Detect Vulnerable Elements on Web Pages and Avoid Clickjacking. Proceedings of the 6th International Conference on Cloud System and Big Data Engineering (Confluence). 14-15 Jan. Noida, India.

Pearlson K.E., Saunders C.S. and Galletta D.F. (2016). Managing and Using Information System, Binder Ready Version: A Strategic Approach. Wiley.

Prabha K. and Sree S.S. (2016). A Survey on IPS Methods and Techniques, International Journal of Computer Science Issues (IJCSI). 13(2). pp.38-43.

Psiaki M.L. and Humphreys T.E. (2016). GNSS Spoofing and Detection, Proceedings of the IEEE. 104(8). pp.1258-1270.

Raggad B.G. (2010). Information Security Management: Concepts and Practice. CRC Press

Rakitin S.R. (2016). What Can Software Quality Engineering Contribute to Cyber Security? Software Quality Professional Magazine.

Romney, M.B., Steinbart P.J. (2015). Accounting Information Systems. Boston: Pearson.

Rostami M., Koushanfar F., Rajendran J. and Karri R. (2013). Hardware Security: Threat Models and Metrics. Proceedings of IEEE /ACM International Conference on Computer-Aided Design, Digest of Technical Papers, Nov.

Sathya A., Swetha J., Das K.A. and George K.K. (2016). Robust Features for Spoofing Detection, International Conference on Advances in Computing, Communication and Informatics (ICACCI'2016). 21-24 June. Jaipur.

Scannell K. (2016), Cyber Crime: How Companies are Hit by Email Scams, Financial Times, 24 February. (accessed 11 Nov 2016).

Selim H., Tayeb S., Kim Y., Zhan J. and Pirouz M. (2016). Vulnerability Analysis of Iframe Attack on Websites. Proceedings of the 3rd Multidisciplinary International Social Networks Conference on Social Informatics. ACM Digital Library. 15-17 Aug.

Shahriar H. and Haddad H.M. (2015). Client-Side Detection of Clickjacking Attacks, International Journal of Information Security and Privacy. 9(1), p.25.

Shen Y., Evans N. and Benameur A. (2016). Insights into rooted and non-rooted Android Mobile Devices with Behavior Analytics. Proceedings of the 31st Annual ACM Symposium on Applied Computing. 4-8 April. Pisa, Italy. pp.580-587.

Shim J., Qureshi A.A., Siegel J.G. (2013). The International Handbook of Computer Security. New York: Routledge, p.33.

Silva A.S., Dos Santos R.C., Bottura F.B. and Oleskovicz M. (2017). Development and Evaluation of a Prototype for Remote Voltage Monitoring Based on Artificial Neural Network. Journal of Engineering Applications of Artificial Intelligence, vol.57, pp.50-60.

Singh B. and Panda S.N. (2015). A Proactive Approach to Intrusion Detection in Cloud Software as a Service. In: Achieving Enterprise Agility Through Innovative Software Development. IGI Publisher.

Solms R.V. and NieKerk J.V. (2013). From Information Security to Cyber Security, Issue: Cybercrime in the Digital Economy, Journal of Computers, and Security. vol.38. pp.97-102.

Sushama R., Borhade, Sandip A. and Kahate (2016). Detection of Backdoor Attacks with Generating Alerts Over Mobile Networks. International Journal of Engineering Sciences & Management Research. 3(5). pp.37-42.

Stede W.V. and Malone R. (2010). Accounting Trends in a Borderless World, Chartered Institute of Management Accountants. No: 1859716903.

Tyagi, A.K. (2016). Cyber Physical Systems (CPSs) - Opportunities and Challenges for Improving Cyber Security. International Journal of Computer Applications. 137(14). p.19.

Ward J. and Peppard J. (2016). The Strategic Management of Information Systems: Building a Digital Strategy. Wiley.

Keskin S., Erdogan H.T. and Kocak T. (2016). Graphics Processing Unit Based Next Generation DDoS Prevention System, Proceedings of 4th International Symposium on Digital Forensic and Security (ISDFS'16). 24-25 April. Little Rock, Arkanasa, USA.

Khan H.M., Chan G.Y. and Chua F.F. (2016). An Adaptive Monitoring Framework for Ensuring Accountability and Quality of Services in Cloud Computing. Proceedings of 30th International Conference on Information Networking (ICOIN'16). 13-15 Jan. Kota Kinabalu, Malaysia.

Rouvinen, J.T. (2015). Detection of a Threat in a Communications Network. 8 Dec. US Patent: 9208311B2.

Wang C., Chow S.S.M, Wang Q. and Ren K. (2013). Privacy-preserving Public Auditing for Secure Cloud Storage. IEEE Transactions on Computers. 62(2). pp.362-375.

Wikipedia (2016). List of Countries by Number of Mobile Phones in Use. (accessed on 29 Oct 2016).

Wong, Y.K. (2016). Modern Software Review: Techniques and Technologies, IGI Global.

Wong Y. K., Rubasinghe A., and Steele R.J. (2005). An Empirical Research Program for Biometric Technology Adoption, Proceedings of the IRIS'28 Conference. Kristiansand, Norway, pp.6-9.

Wong Y.K. and Thite M. (2009). Information Security and Privacy in Human Resources Information Systems. Sega Publisher. pp.395-407.

Wong Y.K. (2003). An Exploratory Study of Software Review in Practice, Portland International Conference on Management of Engineering and Technology (PICMET'03). Technology Management for Reshaping the World, pp.301-308, IEEE Publisher.

Worldometers (2016), Real Time World Statistics, worldometers.com (accessed 7 Dec 2016)

Xing X., Meng W., Lee B., Weinsberg U. and Sheth A. (2015) Understanding Malvertising Through Ad-injecting Browser Extensions. Proceedings of the 24th International Conference on World Wide Web (WWW'15). Florence, Italy. 18-15 May, pp. 1286-1295.

Yan Q., Yu F.R., Gong Q. and Li J. (2016) Software-defined Networking (SDN) and Distributed Denial of Service (DDoS) Attacks in Cloud Computing Environments: A Survey, Some Research Issues and Challenges, IEEE Communications Surveys and Tutorials, 18(1), pp.602-622.

Yue J., Ma C., Yu H. and Zhou W. (2013). Secrecy-based Access Control for Device-to-Device Communication Under-laying Cellular Network, IEEE Communication Letter, 17(11), pp. 2068-2071.

Zou Y. and Wang G. (2016). Intercept Behavior Analysis Industrial Wireless Sensor Networks in Presence of Eavesdropping Attack, IEEE Transactions on Industrial Informatics. 12(2). pp.780-787.

www.ingramcontent.com/pod-product-compliance
Lightning Source LLC
Chambersburg PA
CBHW061231180526
45170CB00003B/1248